Protecting

Our Feathered Friends

Protecting
Our Feathered Friends

by Dean T. Spaulding

Lerner Publications Company • Minneapolis

To my family and friends, for putting up with my hobby for all these years.

Photo Acknowledgments

Photos copyrighted to and reproduced with the permission of: Todd Fink/Daybreak Imagery, pp. 2, 45; Dean T. Spaulding, pp. 6, 9, 21, 35, 41 (both); Courtesy Abbeville Press, pp. 11, 14; O'Neill & O'Neill Nature Photography, p. 16; Archive Photos, pp. 19, 24 (Crady Von Pawlak); Rob Curtis/The Early Birder, pp. 22, 48; The Peregrine Fund, p. 27; Ron Garrison/San Diego Zoo, p. 30; Richard Day/Daybreak Imagery, pp. 36, 47, 53; Operation Migration, p. 43.

Front and back cover photographs courtesy of Dean T. Spaulding.

Page 2: A banded Kentucky warbler

Library of Congress Cataloging–in–Publication Data

Spaulding, Dean T.
   Protecting our feathered friends / Dean T. Spaulding
     p. cm. — (Birder's bookshelf)
   Includes index.
   Summary: Describes bird species that are extinct or endangered and efforts by scientists, governments, and organizations to protect endangered birds. Includes step-by-step instructions for projects that readers can do to help local birds, such as building birdfeeders, birdhouses, and birdbaths.
    ISBN 0-8225-3178-X (alk. paper)
   1. Birds, Protection of — Juvenile literature. [1. Birds — Protection. 2. Rare animals. 3. Endangered species.] I. Title. II. Series: Spaulding, Dean T. Birder's bookshelf.
   QL676.5.S663 1997
   598 — dc20
                                          96-25117

Manufactured in the United States of America
1 2 3 4 5 6 – JR – 02 01 00 99 98 97

CONTENTS

Ring-billed gulls in flight, upstate New York

Chapter 1

Here Today...

Extinction—sometimes I wish I'd never heard the word. Sometimes I wish it was not in the dictionary. Perhaps you have run across the word extinction in a book, magazine, or nature program on TV. When we say that an animal or plant is extinct, we mean that all the animals or plants of its kind have died. Extinction is permanent. A creature that becomes extinct will never walk, fly, or swim again. All living things can become extinct, including our feathered friends, the birds.

Does it really matter if a bird becomes extinct? Does it matter if a certain kind of falcon no longer flies through the skies? Does a bird's disappearance affect our lives? The answer to these questions is yes.

Birds give us more than bright feathers and pretty songs on warm spring days. Some birds help control pests. Each year, insects and rodents eat and destroy many acres of crops. Birds help humans by feeding on insects and other pests. Scavengers, birds and other animals that eat dead animals, help keep the environment clean. Vultures are scavengers, as are seagulls.

Birds help plants reproduce by spreading seeds. Blue jays, for example, store acorns as a winter food supply. But the blue jays don't eat all the acorns. Some of them eventually sprout and grow into oak trees. Other birds spread seeds through their excrement, better known as bird droppings. Hummingbirds spread pollen—tiny particles that play a role in plant reproduction—when they travel from flower to flower, drinking nectar.

Extinction Is Natural

Although we may sometimes wish extinction did not exist, in reality, extinction is natural. It has been happening on earth for millions of years. In nature, one species (a specific type of animal or plant) might be stronger, better at finding food, or more aggressive in finding a place to build a nest than another species. The stronger species might survive while the other, weaker species dies out and becomes extinct. This process is called natural selection.

If extinction is natural, then why are we so concerned about species becoming extinct? In past eras, species became extinct at a slow rate—over tens of thousands of years. In modern times, because of pollution, poisonous chemicals, hunting, and destruction of habitats—places where animals naturally live—extinction is happening very rapidly. Many species have become extinct within less than a hundred years. People who are working to protect birds and other animals would like to slow extinction down to its natural rate.

In *Protecting Our Feathered Friends,* you will learn about birds that have become extinct. You will also learn about birds that are close to extinction and how people are trying to save them. Finally, you will learn ways that you, too, can help protect our feathered friends.

Volunteers with a newborn black-crowned night-heron. Only trained people are allowed to handle wild birds.

Chapter 2

Gone Forever

Prior to the 20th century, people thought of most birds as a source of food. People shot many kinds of birds and ate them. People also ate birds' eggs.

Even many birders, people who watch birds as a hobby, sometimes shot and killed the birds they saw. The dead birds were identified, stuffed, and kept in collections.

Some birds were killed because they were pretty. In the 18th and 19th centuries, birds such as egrets, herons, and terns were killed for their long, elegant feathers—called plumes. Most plumes were shipped to Europe, where they were put onto fashionable hats for women.

Within a short time, many species became extinct. These birds are gone, but we can learn from their stories.

Passenger pigeons, painted by John James Audubon, before the species was hunted to extinction.

The Passenger Pigeon

The last passenger pigeon was a female. She died in a zoo in Cincinnati, Ohio, in 1914. Her name was Martha Washington.

A hundred years before Martha Washington died, more passenger pigeons lived in North America than any other kind of bird. Passenger pigeons nested, or raised their young, in large colonies. The largest known colony, located in Wisconsin, was home to more than 135 million adult passenger pigeons.

The passenger pigeon became extinct for one reason: overhunting. Passenger pigeon meat was tasty, and many Americans

enjoyed eating it. People particularly liked the meat of young passenger pigeons growing in their nests. These young birds were called squabs.

Adult passenger pigeons were shot with guns, but squabs were not shot. Instead, hunters waited for passenger pigeons to make their nests, lay eggs, and hatch them. (Passenger pigeons laid one egg per nest.) When the squabs were a few weeks old, hunters would simply cut down the trees that held the nests. They would collect the squabs from the ground, kill them, and ship them off to market.

As whole colonies of passenger pigeons were destroyed, people finally began to take notice. In 1867, New York State passed a law making it illegal to kill passenger pigeons. Several other states passed similar laws. But these efforts came too late. The passenger pigeon population was already very low, and the birds became extinct.

If you want to see a passenger pigeon, you'll have to go to a science museum and look at a dead one that has been stuffed and preserved. You could also look at the paintings of artist John James Audubon. One of his books, *The Birds of America,* includes a painting of two passenger pigeons. Another way to get a sense of what the passenger pigeon looked like is to look at its relative the mourning dove. Mourning doves are found throughout the United States and Canada. They are not in danger of extinction.

The Great Auk

The great auk lived on and around the northern Atlantic Ocean. It was a large bird with dark black plumage, or feathers, and a thick black bill, or beak. The great auk stood upright, much like a penguin does. It was an excellent diver. It could dive more than 250 feet below the water's surface to catch fish.

Although the great auk moved well in the water, it didn't move well on land. In the air, the great auk didn't move at all. It was a flightless bird. Like the passenger pigeon, the great auk nested in large colonies. Because they couldn't fly, great auks did not build nests in trees but instead nested on rocky ocean shores.

The auk colonies were easy pickings for sailors in the North Atlantic. Sailors collected auk eggs and killed auks for their meat and feathers. Young auks were used as fish bait. Eventually, only a few auks remained. Some of the last ones were killed by bird collectors who wanted their skins. On June 3, 1844, the last known great auk was killed in Iceland.

The Carolina Parakeet

The Carolina parakeet was the only species of parrot native to North America. Parrots are colorful birds with thick beaks and brightly colored feathers. You may have seen a parrot or parakeet at a pet store.

The Carolina parakeet had green, yellow, and red feathers on its upper body. It was a social bird that traveled during the day in large flocks. At night, Carolina parakeets slept inside cavities (hollows) in decaying trees. They also nested and raised their young inside tree cavities.

Because people liked the Carolina parakeet's beautiful coloring, some of the birds were caged and sold as pets. Because they ate crops, farmers considered them to be pests and shot them in large numbers. Eventually, the birds were hunted to extinction. The last Carolina parakeet died in the Cincinnati Zoo in 1914.

Audubon's painting of the Labrador duck

The Labrador Duck

The Labrador duck was named for Labrador, Canada, where it nested. The male had a brightly colored bill and attractive black and white feathers.

The Labrador duck became extinct so quickly that some people did not believe it ever existed. But John James Audubon did. Audubon painted the duck after a trip to Canada.

People hunted Labrador ducks for food and collected and ate their eggs. The duck became extinct in the 1870s. All we have left to remind us of this bird are its skins (some of which are stuffed and displayed in museums) and Audubon's painting of the Labrador duck.

Chapter 3

Changing Direction

For many years, few people worried about extinction. Perhaps people thought there would always be more animals, no matter how many were killed.

In the late 19th century, scientific knowledge was growing. Naturalists, or field biologists, began to collect, study, and catalog different types of animals. They wanted to learn what food the animals ate, how they raised their young, and which species were related to each other.

Naturalists began to notice that some species of birds and animals were declining in numbers. There was a new interest not only in understanding animals but also in helping them.

In 1886, a New York naturalist named George Bird Grinnell formed a group dedicated to saving the lives of birds and other animals. Grinnell named this group the Audubon Society, in honor of John James Audubon.

A great egret

Soon, naturalists in other states got involved in the society's work. In 1895 Audubon societies formed in Pennsylvania and Massachusetts. Gradually, more state societies formed. In 1905, they joined together as the National Association of Audubon Societies. (In 1935, the name was shortened to National Audubon Society.)

Working with state and local governments, Audubon societies pushed for laws that helped protect birds and other animals. First, Audubon societies focused on the plume trade. In 1911, the Audubon Act was passed in New York State. This law made it illegal to sell the feathers of wild birds in New York. In 1913, the Tariff Act, a national law, made it illegal for Americans to export wild bird feathers to European markets. This law finally brought an end to the plume trade in the United States.

The great egret, whose numbers had been rapidly decreasing because of the plume trade, was saved from extinction. The great egret became the Audubon Society symbol.

Another important law was the Migratory Bird Treaty Act, passed in 1918. This law made hunting most kinds of wild birds illegal. It also regulated the hunting of game birds, such as ducks and turkeys.

Silent Spring

The use of insecticides, chemicals that kill insects, has harmed many bird species. Insecticides keep insects from eating crops. Unfortunately, these chemicals do more than just kill bugs. Insecticides also hurt—and sometimes kill—birds.

The most harmful insecticide to birds is dichloro-diphenyl-trichloroethane, or DDT, first used in the early 1940s. In the 1960s, ornithologists, scientists who study birds, began to notice that the populations of certain bird species were dropping. Numbers of bald eagles and peregrine falcons were becoming very low. The cause was DDT.

After it was sprayed on crops, DDT ran off into rivers and lakes. Fish and other animals that live in water took DDT into their bodies when they swam and ate. When birds ate fish containing DDT, the DDT ended up in the birds' body fat.

Birds reproduce by laying and hatching eggs. Adult birds must incubate eggs, or keep them warm, as the young birds inside the eggs grow. Birds keep eggs warm by sitting on them.

DDT damaged birds' eggs. It made egg shells very thin—so thin that the eggs cracked when adult birds sat on them. Fewer eggs hatched, fewer birds were born, and bald eagles, peregrine falcons, and some other birds became "endangered species." An endangered species is a plant or animal that is in danger of becoming extinct.

Rachel Carson, a biologist and writer, took a close look at DDT and how it affected birds. Her famous book, published in 1962, was titled *Silent Spring*. The book warned about the dangers of DDT and about a world without musical birdsongs. Thanks in part to Carson's book, DDT was banned in the United States, Canada, and many other countries in 1972.

Unfortunately, DDT was not banned everywhere around the world. Birds that live in North America in summer often migrate, or travel, to countries in Central and South America in winter. In some of these countries, DDT is still used to kill mosquitoes and other insects. As a result, DDT still threatens migrating birds such as the peregrine falcon.

The Endangered Species Act

In 1973, the United States Congress passed a law to help protect and restore endangered species—both plants and animals. Under the Endangered Species Act, the U.S. Fish and Wildlife Service determines which species are in danger of extinction and develops programs to help protect them.

The Fish and Wildlife Service keeps an endangered species list. The national list includes about 90 birds. Each state also has an endangered species list, although a state listing doesn't necessarily mean that a species is endangered on the national level.

Biologist Rachel Carson called attention to the dangers of insecticides such as DDT. Here, Carson fills a bird feeder with seed.

There is no specific population count that designates a bird as endangered. Some endangered species have a few thousand individual birds; others have less than 100. (By contrast, birds that aren't endangered might number in the hundreds of thousands.) Endangered species are designated on a case-by-case basis.

When the population of an endangered species increases to the point where the species no longer needs help from humans, the species is said to be "recovered." Recovered species are removed from the endangered species list. But they are not forgotten. Species that are not officially endangered but whose numbers are still low are called "threatened." Often, recovered

species are placed on the threatened species list. Scientists watch threatened species closely to make sure that their numbers do not decrease further.

Wildlife Refuges

Around the world, bird habitats are also threatened. In many places, wetlands, fields, and forests—places where birds build nests, spend winters, and stop off during migration—have been drained and cleared. People have built houses, offices, farms, and roads in these places. Without their usual nesting spots and wintering grounds, birds cannot survive.

To reverse this trend, many governments around the world have set aside certain habitats as wildlife refuges, or sanctuaries. No one can build houses or roads in these places. They are protected by law. The National Wildlife Refuge System includes more than 400 refuges run by the U.S. government. States and private organizations also run wildlife refuges. The Audubon Society runs more than 100 sanctuaries on more than 250,000 acres of American wilderness.

Though these places are maintained especially for birds and other wildlife, people are allowed in, too. Refuges are great places for bird-watchers, photographers, and anyone else who wants to enjoy nature.

Many habitats have been set aside as wildlife refuges.

The whooping crane is one of many endangered birds in the United States.
The population of whooping cranes stands at about 300.

Chapter 4

Back from the Brink

In 1782, the bald eagle became the national bird of the United States. Two hundred years later, the bald eagle was endangered. So were many other kinds of birds. Scientists and government agencies went to work. The effort to save our feathered friends would involve both hard work and clever thinking.

The Bald Eagle

The bald eagle is a large bird of prey (a bird that kills small animals for food). It has white feathers on its tail and head. When viewed from a distance, the eagle looks bald.

Though bald eagles sometimes eat ducks, rabbits, and seabirds, they mainly eat fish. Eagles have excellent eyesight (that's where the phrase "eagle eye" comes from). Soaring high above the water, eagles search for fish swimming below the surface. Once an eagle spots a fish, it dives down and snatches it from the water, using its sharp talons, or claws. The eagle flies off to eat the fish in a quiet spot.

Bald eagles usually build their nests in tall pine trees. Many eagles use the same nests year after year—for 10 years or more in some cases. But, by the 1970s, many pine trees in the United States had been cut down for lumber. Eagles had to abandon their traditional nesting places and look for new ones. Many eagles did not nest for several years after their homes were destroyed. The eagle population began to decline.

There were more reasons for the decline. Some bald eagles were electrocuted when they flew into power lines. Others were

A bald eagle

killed by illegal hunting. Finally, DDT had also damaged the eagle population.

In 1978, the bald eagle was placed on the national endangered species list. By 1982, there were fewer than 1,500 eagle pairs nesting in the United States, not including Alaska (where the bird was not endangered).

What could people do to help the bald eagle? Several efforts were begun. One was the captive-breeding program organized by the U.S. Fish and Wildlife Service. In this program, pairs of bald eagles were placed in large cages, where they mated, laid eggs, and raised young.

Once the young eagles were old enough to fly and take care of themselves, they were released into the wild with radio monitors attached to their legs. The monitors did not harm the birds. They just allowed scientists to track the eagles' movements using radio signals. In this way, scientists learned more about the eagles' migration patterns, nesting habits, and habitats. The more the scientists could learn about bald eagles, the more they could help them.

In many states, universities and government agencies established rehabilitation centers. Rehabilitation centers are a lot like hospitals for birds and other wild animals. Injured eagles that would otherwise have died were treated at rehabilitation centers and released back into the wild. Educational programs increased public awareness about bald eagles and helped cut down on illegal hunting. Power lines were redesigned so that birds that accidentally flew into them would not be electrocuted.

All the hard work paid off. In 1995, the bald eagle was taken off the federal endangered species list.

The Peregrine Falcon

The peregrine falcon used to be called the duck hawk because it often eats ducks (though it eats other kinds of birds, too). It has large, pointed wings and a dark head area, or hood. When stooping, flying down through the sky to catch prey, peregrine falcons can reach speeds up to 200 miles per hour.

In the 1930s and 1940s, about 1,000 pairs of peregrine falcons lived in the entire United States. How do we know this number? Peregrine falcons often nest on cliff ledges, using the same ledges year after year. These sites are called "historical nesting sites." Because falcons nest in the same places each year, it isn't very difficult for scientists to find peregrines, count them, and monitor their breeding habits.

By the 1960s, not a single pair of peregrine falcons was breeding in the eastern United States and most were gone in the western United States. The spraying of insecticides such as DDT had brought the peregrine very close to extinction.

The banning of DDT in the United States helped the peregrine begin to recover. In addition, in 1970, scientists at Cornell University, working with state and federal agencies, began a project called the Peregrine Fund. Through this project, more than 4,500 peregrine falcons have been bred in captivity and released into the wild.

By the early 1990s, peregrine numbers were looking good and climbing. The population is about as high as it was in the 1940s—about 1,000 pairs live in the lower 48 states. Peregrines are doing so well, in fact, that the bird might be moved from the endangered species list to the threatened list.

Peregrine falcons are carefully monitored all over the United

A peregrine falcon with chicks

States. Scientists watch nesting sites and track the birds with radio monitors. If numbers drop again, scientists want to be able to react quickly.

The Piping Plover

The piping plover—a shorebird with yellow legs and feet and a bright orange, black-tipped bill—was hunted around the turn of the century. Before long, its numbers became very low, though precise figures were not recorded in the early 1900s. In 1918 Congress passed the Migratory Bird Treaty Act. The hunting of wild birds was outlawed, and the piping plover was able to recover.

But the species is back in trouble. This time, it's not gunshots that are bringing down numbers of piping plovers. It's people going to the beach who are hurting the birds.

Piping plovers make their nests on the ground. They prefer grassy areas and dunes near beaches. But plovers have no way of protecting their nests if someone, or something, comes traveling through the dunes. At the beach, both people and pets bother plovers and their nests. When people walk or drive off-road vehicles through the dunes, or build nearby beach homes, plovers abandon their nests, eggs, and young.

In 1985, the piping plover became an endangered species in many of the states where it breeds. It was also an endangered species in Canada.

To help the piping plover, conservation groups such as the Audubon Society and the Nature Conservancy used an important tool: education. The groups put up posters with information about piping plovers. They cautioned people not to walk through dunes when plovers were raising their young and asked them to keep pets on leashes at the beach.

On some beaches, conservation groups placed wire mesh around piping plovers' nests. The holes in the mesh are large enough that parent plovers can walk through them to care for their young. But large animals such as seagulls can't get through the mesh to harm the young plovers. The mesh also protects the nest from people. Thanks to such efforts, the number of piping plovers is increasing.

The Whooping Crane

Whooping cranes are interesting to look at. They are white birds with long legs and long necks. They have red faces and red feathers on the top of their heads. They get their name from their call, a loud trumpeting sound.

People hunted whooping cranes, beginning in the late 1800s. The 1918 Migratory Bird Treaty Act put an end to the hunting. But, by then, numbers were already very low. By 1941, only about 20 whooping cranes remained in the United States.

Loss of habitat also contributed to the whooping cranes' disappearance. Whooping cranes used to live in a number of different places in the United States. They made their nests in quiet prairie marshes. But as Americans built more houses, farms, and shopping centers, whooping cranes had fewer places to live and raise their young. Since the 1940s, whooping cranes have wintered mainly in the 74-square-mile Aransas National Wildlife Refuge in Texas. In spring, the birds fly 2,500 miles north until they reach Wood Buffalo National Park in northern Alberta, Canada, where they nest and raise their young.

In the 1970s, ornithologists stepped in to help the whooping cranes. Scientists removed eggs from whooping cranes' nests and placed the eggs in the nests of sandhill cranes. The sandhill cranes then hatched and raised the young whooping cranes. This switch did not bother the whooping cranes. They simply laid another clutch (group of eggs) and hatched those eggs instead. By this method, more whooping cranes were able to be raised each season.

Unfortunately, the project didn't work as well as scientists had hoped. Whooping cranes that were raised by sandhill cranes did not breed when they reached adulthood. The project failed, and scientists looked for other ways to help whooping cranes, such as protecting their breeding and wintering grounds. The whooping crane population has increased to about 300, but the species is still in trouble.

The California Condor

The California condor, a member of the vulture family, is one of the rarest birds in the United States. It is also the largest. It can measure 10 feet from wing to wing. Condors are scavengers. They eat dead and decaying animals.

California condors once lived throughout much of the United States. By the early 1900s, the condors were found only in southern California and the Baja Peninsula. Eventually, they lived in just one valley in southern California. By 1986, only three birds remained in the wild (although 27 were living in captivity).

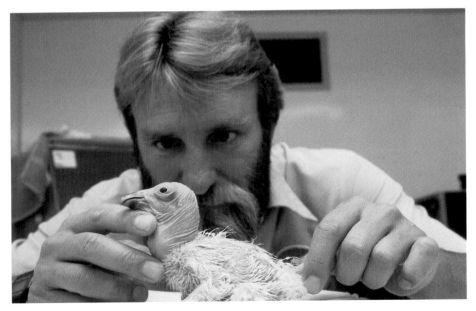

A scientist from the Condor Recovery Program weighs a one-day-old condor chick.

The California condor population had declined for several reasons. Many condors were accidentally killed when they ate poisoned bait left by ranchers to kill coyotes. Condors also reproduce very slowly. Most birds begin reproducing when they are just a year old. Condors can't breed until age eight, and typically they have only one chick every two years. As a result, very few condors are born each year.

In the late 1980s, scientists formed the Condor Recovery Program. Working with the San Diego Wild Animal Park and the Los Angeles Zoo, scientists bred and raised condors in captivity. Later, the three condors that remained in the wild were captured. The wild condors and the condors raised by humans were bred. By 1996, according to the U.S. Fish and Wildlife Service, 100 California condors were living in captivity. Also by this time, about 17 young condors born in captivity were released back into the wild.

Unfortunately, many of the birds did not survive. Of the condors reintroduced into the wild, only a few are still flying free. Even these condors aren't exactly "free," since they are still being monitored via radio by the Condor Recovery Program. Until the California condor can exist on its own, without the aid of humans, many people wonder about the fate of these great birds.

The Kirtland's Warbler

The Kirtland's warbler is a yellow-breasted bird with a bluish gray back. It is about five inches long and, like other members of the warbler family, it eats mainly insects. The bird nests mostly in northern Michigan in spring and summer and spends winters in the Bahamas.

The Kirtland's warbler is one of the rarest songbirds in the United States. This wasn't always the case. In the late 1800s, approximately 2,000 pairs of Kirtland's warblers were breeding in northern Michigan.

Thoughout the 20th century, numbers began to decline. In 1951, scientists counted only 432 male Kirtland's warblers. In 1987, the number of males was down to 167. (Scientists count Kirtland's warblers by listening for the male's song.)

Why the big drop in numbers? Surprisingly, the decline wasn't due to people building superhighways or big shopping centers. It was caused, in part, by a drop in forest fires.

The Kirtland's warbler makes its nest on the ground. Low-hanging branches of jack pine, a kind of pine tree, protect the nest. Jack pine grows very quickly, and in five years or so becomes too big to provide protection to nesting warblers.

But nature creates new jack pines for the Kirtland's warbler. When forest fires burn an area, old jack pines are killed, and new ones grow in their place. People, of course, try to put out forest fires.

Because of firefighting efforts in northern Michigan, old jack pines were not being replaced by young ones. The Kirtland's warbler no longer had the special type of habitat it needed for nesting, and its numbers began to drop.

The U.S. Fish and Wildlife Service, the U.S. Forest Service, and the Michigan Department of Natural Resources are working together to help the Kirtland's warbler. These groups set *controlled* fires in old jack pine forests in northern Michigan. Afterward, land is cleared and—to speed up the regrowing process—new jack pines are planted. Scientists also remove cowbirds, a species

that destroys other birds' eggs, from the Kirtland's warblers' habitat.

This work has been successful. In 1994, scientists counted 633 male Kirtland's warblers.

Puffins and Terns

Puffins are ocean birds. Three species of puffins live in North America. The Atlantic puffin is found on the East Coast.

Atlantic puffins have wide, brightly colored bills. They dive to catch fish, fly, walk, and swim. They stand up straight, sort of like humans do.

Many people love puffins. People even buy puffin memorabilia—items such as T-shirts, jewelry, and cards with pictures of puffins on them. But many people don't know that for about 100 years, no Atlantic puffins nested in the United States.

Atlantic puffins once lived on Egg Rock Island and other islands off the coast of northern Maine. During the 19th century, hunters killed the puffins on Egg Rock for food and for their feathers. Three kinds of terns—common, Arctic, and roseate—lived on Egg Rock Island too. The terns were hunted for their tail feathers, and their eggs were gathered and eaten. By about 1880, puffins and terns were gone from Egg Rock Island.

In 1969, ornithologist Stephen Kress led a bird-watching class near Egg Rock Island. He was disappointed that the puffins were gone, and he wondered whether he could return them to the island.

Puffins were not an endangered species. There were still large puffin colonies in Canada. So Kress took six young puffins from a colony in Canada and brought them to Egg Rock Island.

Puffins raise their young inside burrows, holes in the ground. At Egg Rock Island, puffins had once used deep crevices between rocks as burrows. Kress made imitation burrows between blocks of sod and placed the young puffins inside them. A few times a day, he dropped in fish to feed the young birds, just like a parent puffin would have.

At about two months old, the puffins left their burrows and headed out to sea. Puffins spend their first two or three years swimming on the ocean, feeding on fish.

Kress hoped the puffins would remember Egg Rock Island once they were fully grown and would return there to nest and raise their young. But puffins and other seabirds nest only where other birds of their kind are nesting. That way, they know an area is safe for raising a family.

Since there were no longer any puffins nesting normally on Egg Rock Island, Kress built puffin decoys—fake puffins made out of wood. He hoped the real puffins would see the decoys and know the island was safe for nesting.

Kress continued to raise puffin chicks on the island each summer. Finally, on June 12, 1977—four years after the first hand-raised puffins left Egg Rock—puffins began to return to the island. In 1981 they began nesting there.

In 1974, Kress decided to try and return terns to Egg Rock Island, too. Unlike puffins, terns nest in the open, right on the ground. If Kress had left tern chicks in the open on Egg Rock, they would have quickly fallen prey to a hungry bird such as a black-backed gull.

So Kress tried another approach. He built wooden decoys that looked like terns, set them up on the island, and played tern-

These birds are decoys. The one on the right looks like a razorbill and the two on the left like puffins. They are set up to attract these two kinds of birds to Egg Rock Island.

colony noises—mating calls and loud chatters—on tape. Nearby terns were tricked into thinking that a tern colony existed on Egg Rock and that it was a safe place for nesting.

By 1981, common terns, Arctic terns, and endangered roseate terns were all nesting on Egg Rock Island. People can now take a "puffin cruise" past Egg Rock and nearby islands and see the puffins and terns for themselves.

The method that Kress used with the puffins and terns has been copied by other ornithologists. By moving young birds to new sites and by using decoys, scientists have reintroduced and increased the numbers of about 30 species of endangered seabirds.

Two Sides of the Story

Most people agree that helping endangered and threatened birds is a good idea. But making a good idea work is not always easy. Often, when it comes to protecting endangered species, the needs of humans and the needs of animals are not the same.

The northern spotted owl lives in the Pacific Northwest (northern California, Oregon, Washington, and British Columbia) in a special habitat called old-growth forest. Most old-growth forest in the United States is on public land, which is managed by the U.S. government.

The northern spotted owl needs large tracts of old-growth forest in which to breed. Logging companies rely on old-growth forests, too. These forests supply lumber that people use in building homes and products. But, by cutting down old-growth forests, logging companies also destroy the northern spotted owl's habitat.

In June 1990, the northern spotted owl was listed as a threatened species. To protect the owl, wildlife conservationists wanted to protect the old-growth forest. They wanted to restrict logging on millions of acres of federally owned old-growth forest in the Pacific Northwest.

Logging companies were opposed to the idea. They argued that if public lands were closed to logging, then paper mills, sawmills, lumber yards, and other businesses would be hurt or forced to close. Loggers would lose their jobs.

The debate received widespread media attention. In January 1992, the U.S. Fish and Wildlife Service announced that approximately 7 million acres of old-growth forest would be set aside as protected habitat—with strict limits on logging.

Neither side is entirely happy with the decision. Conservationists worry that not enough land has been set aside for the spotted owl. Logging companies want more land available for logging. Whose needs are more important, the people's or the owl's? It's a complicated question. What do you think?

Chapter 5

Tracking Our Feathered Friends

How do scientists know how many birds of a certain species exist? How do they know when populations increase or decrease? It's simple—by counting them.

Counting birds is not an exact science. But bird counts do give scientists useful estimates of bird populations. Many bird counts are held each year. Some counts involve only one type of bird, such as hawks. Other counts involve birds that are nesting.

Birds such as the peregrine falcon and bald eagle usually nest in the same places year after year. Counting birds is easier when you already know where to find them. Sometimes birds and their nests are harder to spot. So birders count certain birds by listening for the male's song.

During bird counts, people travel in vehicles and on foot. The counters usually use binoculars to get a better view of faraway birds. Modern technology has been a big help to bird counters. During some counts, people even travel in airplanes and helicopters. The view from above lets them spot birds in the middle of large lakes.

The most famous bird count in North America is the Christmas Count, which takes place each year during the Christmas season. During the Christmas Count, people travel through 15-mile-wide "count circles" looking for birds. In 1994, counts were taken at 1,645 circles in the United States and Canada. More than 40,000 birders participated.

After the Christmas Count, participants in each circle gather together and add up the numbers of birds and species they have counted. The National Audubon Society publishes the count totals, comparing the results to previous years' numbers.

Another important bird count, the Breeding Bird Survey, is held each year in June. About 2,000 birders participate. Following an assigned route, they note adult birds, mating songs, and other signs that birds are raising families. By counting breeding birds, ornithologists get a better idea of whether bird populations are growing or declining.

You don't have to be a scientist to join the Christmas Count or a different bird count. Amateur bird-watchers are welcome to help out.

Banding

Another technique ornithologists use to keep track of birds is called banding. Banding involves placing a metal band around a bird's leg. Most bands are made of lightweight stainless steel. They do not bother birds. In fact, the bands are so light that after a few minutes the birds probably forget the bands altogether.

Ornithologists band thousands of birds each year. Most banding takes place at special banding stations, operated by universities, conservation groups, and government wildlife agencies. Bird banding is serious business. People who band birds must have special permits, issued by the U.S. Fish and Wildlife Service.

Ornithologists band birds in several ways. They sometimes band young birds that are ready to leave the nest. These birds are called fledglings. The bander must wait until a fledgling's legs have grown. That way, the band won't be too tight when the bird reaches adulthood.

Other times, ornithologists capture flying birds in special "mist nets," strung up on poles. Mist nets are very thin—so thin that even though birds have good eyesight, they can't see the nets while they're flying.

When a bird is caught, the bander carefully untangles it from the mist net. The bander identifies the bird, measures it, bands it, and writes the information in a logbook. Then the bander releases the bird back into the wild.

If someone finds a banded bird after it dies, the person can send the band and details about the dead bird to the U.S. Fish and Wildlife Service. The USFWS sends the information back to the bird's bander. Sometimes, living banded birds are recaptured.

Most banded birds are never found. But when a banded bird is discovered, scientists get valuable information. How old was the bird when it died? How far had it flown since banding, and where had it gone? By banding, scientists can learn more about

Yellow warbler caught in a mist net. *Right:* Measuring a banded Wilson's warbler.

how birds nest, where they migrate, and what routes they take.

Bird banding stations operate during all seasons, but most banding occurs during spring and fall, when birds are migrating. School groups can take field trips to banding stations. There, students can watch the ornithologists at work and sometimes even help them.

Flying with the Birds

Many birds migrate, or travel, with the seasons. They fly north in spring to reach their breeding grounds. In fall, the birds fly south again to spend the winter in warm places with abundant food supplies.

Some birds migrate solo, or alone. The bald eagle is a good example. Other birds migrate in flocks, or groups. Canada geese are easy to recognize during migration because they fly in a V-shaped formation. In April and May, a flock of geese flying north overhead is a welcome sign of spring. When the geese fly south in October and November, we know that winter isn't far behind.

Most kinds of birds migrate by instinct. Instinct is the natural ability or knowledge that an animal has from the moment it is born. Many migrating birds fly hundreds, even thousands, of miles on instinct. Though they may never have flown the course before, they locate their breeding grounds and wintering grounds with precision.

Some birds—Canada geese, for instance—do not have this kind of instinct for migration. They do not know the course from birth and must be led by an adult bird to their breeding and wintering grounds. Once they are shown the way, however, the geese remember it for the rest of their lives. They go on to show the course to younger birds.

Canada geese that are raised in captivity don't always have adult birds to lead them during migration. Could the

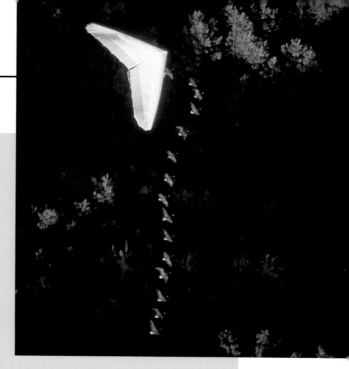

Bill Lishman in flight with his "family" of geese.

humans who raise the birds teach them to migrate? One birder, Bill Lishman of Oshawa, Ontario, wanted to find out.

In the summer of 1994, Lishman raised a flock of Canada geese at his home, where he operates a bird sanctuary. Lishman's work wasn't scientific as much as it was an adventure. He wanted to fly like the birds.

In October 1994, Lishman led the flock of geese on a 350-mile trip to wintering grounds in Virginia. He flew in front of the V formation in an ultralight aircraft called *Goose Leader*. Lishman was the only "parent" the birds had ever known—so they followed him.

At first, scientists laughed at Lishman. They're not laughing anymore. Lishman successfully led the geese to their wintering grounds—along a route they will never forget. Scientists hope to use Lishman's method to help endangered species such as whooping cranes, which also need assistance from an experienced adult during migration.

Chapter 6

You Can Help

You can do a lot to make sure that birds are always here with us. Call a local birding store or ask your science teacher about birding groups, wildlife refuges, banding stations, or rehabilitation centers in your area. Ask if they need volunteers. Get involved in a local bird count.

Write a report about an endangered species or an article for your school newspaper. Educate other people about the importance of protecting our feathered friends.

You might even join a conservation group such as the National Audubon Society. The Audubon Society has more than 550,000 members and 500 chapters around the United States. Members usually focus on their own communities, working to protect local birds and their habitats. Local chapters sponsor lectures, field trips, birding workshops, and other projects. The

An ornithologist bands a Kentucky warbler.

Audubon Society even runs special summer camps where young birders learn more about birding and conservation. Maybe you could be one of them.

Though not everyone can band or breed birds in captivity, you can still help the birds that live in your neighborhood or your yard. You can give birds food, water, and safe places to raise their young. Here are just a few projects that you can do to help our feathered friends.

Make a Bird Feeder

You can buy bird feeders at hardware stores and specialty shops. Or you can make a bird feeder yourself. It's simple and the birds will love it!

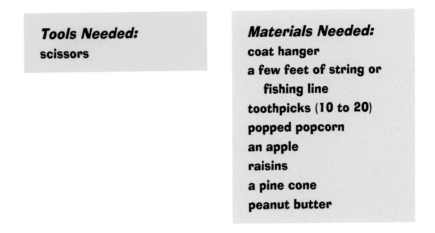

Tools Needed:
scissors

Materials Needed:
coat hanger
a few feet of string or
**   fishing line**
toothpicks (10 to 20)
popped popcorn
an apple
raisins
a pine cone
peanut butter

1. Tie a piece of string or fishing line around the center of an apple. Loop the string crosswise a few times to make sure the apple doesn't slip out. Leave 3 or 4 inches of string hanging.
2. Tie the string or line to the bottom of a coat hanger.
3. Stick toothpicks in the apple
4. Skewer pieces of popped popcorn on the toothpicks.
5. String up a large pine cone next to the apple and coat it with peanut butter.
6. Hang your bird feeder on a tree branch using the hook on the coat hanger.

Sit back and watch the birds that come to eat from your feeder. If you hang the feeder near a window, you can watch the birds from indoors without bothering them.

Replace the popcorn after it's eaten, and every few weeks replace the apple. Try putting raisins on the toothpicks instead of popcorn. String up other kinds of fruit. See what kinds of foods the birds like best.

A northern mockingbird feeds on chokeberries. Many birds eat fruits and berries.

A great-tailed grackle takes a bath.

Make a Birdbath

Birds, like all living things, need water to survive. In nature, our feathered friends drink water from rivers, streams, lakes, ponds, even mud puddles. In winter, if you watch carefully, you can see birds eating snow.

Birds also use water to keep themselves clean. They bathe regularly. Perhaps you've seen a bird take a bath. It dunks itself under the water, rolls the water across its back, then ruffles its feathers rapidly to shake the water off. Bathing birds are fun to watch. Make a birdbath and watch them up close.

Tools Needed:
scissors

Materials Needed:
old tire
large sheet of plastic
    or an old rain poncho
a few buckets of sand
rocks of different sizes

1. Lay the plastic sheet over the tire. The sheet should be big enough to cover the whole tire with excess hanging over the edges.
2. Tuck the excess plastic underneath the tire, but don't stretch it too tight. The plastic should dip down a few inches into the center of the tire.
3. Pour a few inches of clean sand onto the plastic inside the tire. Sand will help the birds keep from slipping on the wet plastic.
4. Add rocks to the sand. Arrange them inside the tire with the biggest ones towards the outside edges.
5. Add about 2 inches of water to the center of the tire. Some of the bigger rocks should stick out of the water. They will make good perches for the birds before and after they bathe.

Put the birdbath in a sunny spot on your lawn. A dark, cold corner of your yard will not be inviting to the birds.

Clean the bath once a month by dumping out the water, sand, and rocks and wiping off any algae that's growing on the plastic. Scrub the plastic with a cleaning brush and vinegar to kill germs.

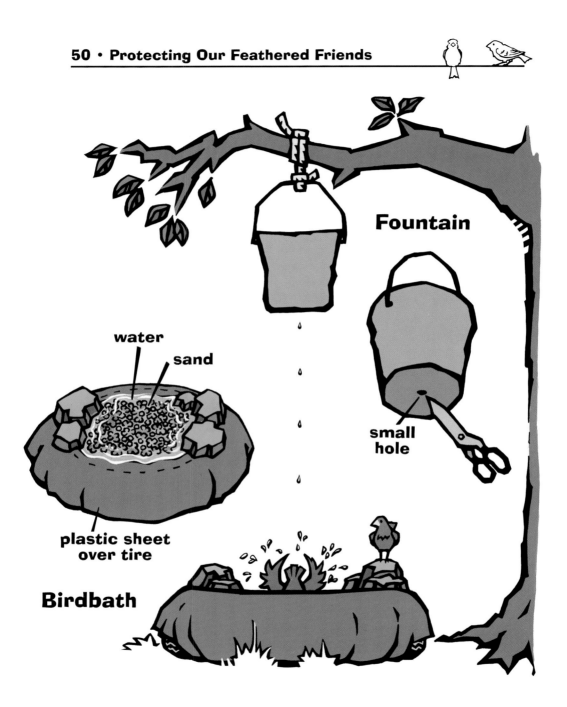

Fountain

water

sand

small hole

plastic sheet over tire

Birdbath

The Birdbath Fountain

The sound of running water will attract even more birds to your yard. Here's how to make the Birdbath Fountain:

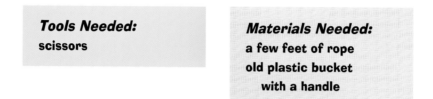

Tools Needed:
scissors

Materials Needed:
a few feet of rope
old plastic bucket
with a handle

1. Take the point of your scissors and make a small hole in the bottom of the plastic container. The hole shouldn't be too big; it should only let water drip out one drop at a time.
2. Tie one end of the rope to the container's handle and the other end to a tree branch above your birdbath. Make sure the knots are tight and the rope is strong.
3. Fill the container with water.

Put your birdbath in a spot where you can easily hang the fountain above the bath. Under a tree limb is best.

Refill the bucket of water whenever it gets empty. Water freezes. So your birdbath and fountain won't work when the temperature is below 32° Fahrenheit. If you live in a place that never gets very cold, keep the bath and fountain full year-round.

Make a Natural Birdhouse

Birdhouses are protective structures in which birds build nests, lay eggs, and raise their young. You can help birds during nesting season by putting birdhouses in your yard. You can buy birdhouses at the store or make them yourself.

A Natural Birdhouse is easy to make. When trees start to decay, they often break apart into sections. A two-foot-long section makes a perfect birdhouse.

Birds that normally raise their young inside holes in decaying trees—birds such as woodpeckers, chickadees, and titmice—will gladly nest inside your Natural Birdhouse. Make several Natural Birdhouses and put them in different places in your yard. Be sure to have them ready in time for nesting season in spring.

Tools Needed:
wire cutter
spoon or garden spade

Materials Needed:
section of decaying tree
trunk
several feet of wire

1. Look for a piece of decaying wood with a little moss on the outside. The moss tells you that the wood inside is soft.
2. Using a spoon or garden tool, make a hole in the middle of the wood. (Be careful not to dig right through to the other side.) The hole should be about 1½ inches wide
3. Reach into the hole with your fingers and remove as much loose wood as you can. You don't have to remove it all. The bird that uses your birdhouse will finish the job.

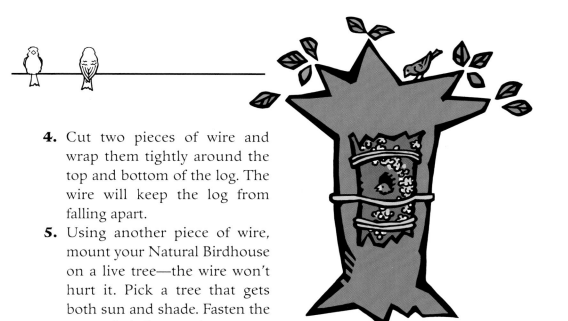

4. Cut two pieces of wire and wrap them tightly around the top and bottom of the log. The wire will keep the log from falling apart.

5. Using another piece of wire, mount your Natural Birdhouse on a live tree—the wire won't hurt it. Pick a tree that gets both sun and shade. Fasten the Natural Birdhouse about 4 or 5 feet off the ground.

Before long, a pair of birds might discover your birdhouse and decide to make a nest there. Watch for birds traveling in and out of the house. But don't get too close or you'll disturb the birds. Keep at least 40 feet away from the house. For a better view, watch the nesting birds through a pair of binoculars.

Woodpeckers might nest in your Natural Birdhouse.

Glossary

banding: affixing a metal band to a bird's leg. Banding allows scientists to study birds' travel and behavior.

endangered species: a species of animal or plant that is threatened with extinction

extinction: the dying out—usually over many generations—of an entire animal or plant species

habitat: the place or environment, such as woods or wetlands, where a plant or animal naturally lives

incubate: to keep eggs in a nest warm enough for the chicks inside to develop and hatch

instinct: a natural ability or knowledge that an animal has from birth

migrate: to move from one location to another, usually to reach new feeding or breeding grounds

natural selection: a process through which species that are strongest or best suited to their environment reproduce and survive while weaker or less adaptable species die out

recovered species: an animal or plant that has been removed from the endangered species list

species: a specific kind of animal within a larger group of similar animals

threatened species: an animal or plant whose numbers are getting low. Threatened species are those that might soon be endangered.

Index

About the Author

Dean T. Spaulding is an environmental journalist and wildlife photographer. His work has appeared in *Audubon, Wild Bird, Birder's World,* and other publications. He is a member and former president of the Adirondack High Peaks Audubon Society and lives in upstate New York.

John Monroe

For more information:
National Audubon Society
700 Broadway
New York, NY 10003
212-979-3000